The Stress
Advantage

LESSONS FROM THE
TENNIS COURT

SHARON GROSSMAN, PHD

WARRIOR
PUBLISHING

Copyright © 2023 by Sharon Grossman, Ph.D.

All rights reserved. No part of this book may be reproduced, distributed, or transmitted in any form or by any means, including photocopying, recording, or other electronic or mechanical methods, without the prior written permission of the publisher, except in the case of brief quotations embodied in critical reviews and certain other noncommercial uses permitted by copyright law. For permission requests, write to the publisher, addressed "Attention: Permission Coordinator," at the address below.

Warrior Publishing, LLC drsharongrossman.com/contact

ISBN 978-1-952437-01-4

Chapter 1: Grab Your Racket 1

Chapter 2: Lace Up Your Sneakers 7

Chapter 3: Play Like a Champion 17

Chapter 4: Game Set Match 25

A Life in Overdrive

In the vibrant town of Springfield, where the rhythm of life echoed through bustling streets and busy schedules, lived Anthony Warfield—a husband, a father of three, and a visionary founder of a thriving construction company known for its sustainable designs.

It was 2 o'clock on a Tuesday, and Anthony found himself in his fifth Zoom meeting of the day. As if the back-to-back meetings weren't enough, an unwelcome headache had decided to crash the party. He leaned back in his chair, rubbing his temples as if he could massage away the stress.

Each day, Anthony's alarm sounds like a starter's pistol, launching him into a frenzied race. From dawn till dusk, he's immersed in a whirlwind of tasks—balancing budgets, making tough decisions, and ensuring his company stays afloat. It's a race against time, but lately, life feels like a never-ending sprint, and he's running out of breath.

Weekends offer little respite. While his family gathers to unwind and enjoy each other's company, Anthony's laptop is a constant companion. He's woven his work into the fabric of his family life. He's justified working on Saturdays as a mere "half day," but even then, he's tethered to his kitchen island, emails pouring in without mercy.

His dedication to his work is undeniable, but it's coming at a cost—precious moments with his loved ones, his health, and his sanity. The TV might play in the background during Sunday evening games, but his mind is often in the office. He enjoys being physically active, but outside of vacations, there seems to be no time for that. When he's lying in bed at night ready to sleep, all too often it takes far longer to turn off his mind than he would like, costing him precious hours of shut eye.

Anthony has inadvertently trained his family to accept his demanding schedule. He's ingrained the idea that working on weekends is part of life, that being "there but not there" is just how things are. Yet, beneath his tough exterior, he can feel the cracks forming.

And it wasn't just the demands, responsibilities, and expectations that were weighing him down. It was the idea that he's "stressed out" that worried him. His father had tragically passed away due to a heart attack, and Anthony couldn't shake the fear that his own stress might lead to similar health issues. He knew he needed to find a way to manage the stress that was accumulating in his life. Unbeknownst to him, Anthony was about to embark on a transformative journey—one that would not only reshape his outlook on challenges but also empower him to harness stress as a catalyst for change.

I invite you to accompany Anthony on his path to rethinking stress through the lessons he learned playing tennis. His story is not just about one man's transformation; it's a reflection of the universal struggles we all face in the modern world. Just as Anthony learned, you'll begin to see that stress isn't the enemy; it's our thinking about stress that can lead us astray. With the right tools, you can change that thinking, develop a more resilient mindset, and uncover the hidden potential within life's challenges.

As you delve into this tale, be prepared to explore stress from a whole new angle. This isn't about wrestling stress to the ground – it's about learning to dance with it. If you're a busy professional seeking a way to manage stress, regain balance, and sidestep burnout, you're about to discover how embracing stress can lead to a brighter, more empowered life.

Chapter 1: Grab Your Racket

Energizing the Game

One day, as he wandered through Springfield's Meadowbrook Park, Anthony stumbled upon a flier advertising tennis lessons. Intrigued, he decided to give it a shot.

A week later, he stepped onto the court, racket in hand. Coach Sarah greeted him with a warm smile. She had a reputation for being a no-nonsense coach who always had a unique perspective on the game. Today, it seemed, would be no different.

Anthony's tennis journey began with a crash course in the basics. Coach Sarah was keen on establishing a strong foundation. She introduced him to the different grips of the racket, emphasizing the importance of keeping a vigilant eye on the ball, and controlling the power of his strokes with finesse.

But then the game sped up. The faster the pace, the more Anthony instinctually tightened up. Sarah noticed Anthony panic as the ball came his way. He had to make quick decisions, and he felt his heartbeat racing and his palms sweating. The more he noticed these physical signs, the more his stress grew as he thought, "I'm so stressed out! This was supposed to be fun."

Right on cue, Coach Sarah stepped in with her racket wisdom. She had seen that deer-in-the-headlights look on many beginners' faces. She gently patted his back and said, "Anthony, when lightning strikes, you can either cower in fear or harness its power. Your body's response to stress, like a bolt of lightning, might make you tremble, but it's also the energy you can use to light up the court." Anthony furrowed his brow, trying to decipher her metaphor.

"Just like a lightning rod channels that energy safely," she continued, "you can learn to channel your physiological symptoms – the racing heart, the adrenaline surge – into an electrifying performance."

Anthony couldn't help but smile, a glimmer of understanding dawning in his eyes. The court was no longer just a battleground; it was a gateway to his thunderous potential.

Those familiar feelings of stress would also creep in as he faced the demands of his work and personal life. That night, as he found himself sifting through emails that seemed to multiply with each passing minute, he felt the telltale signs of stress. His heart quickened, his mind raced, and he could practically hear the buzz of his own thoughts. It was in this moment that he realized he was standing at a crossroads — a pivotal moment where he could apply the lessons from tennis to manage stress and anxiety more effectively.

Instead of panicking, he harnessed the energy his body had produced. He reminded himself that the surge was his body's way of priming him for the challenge, just as it had been on the tennis court. He proceeded to channel that energy to fuel his confidence and strategically tackle his inbox.

As you read Anthony story, think about your own moments of stress. How can you see the energy surge in a positive light?

Instead of feeling worried, how can you use that energy to help you face challenges? Just like Anthony, you can learn to take that energy and turn it into a powerful force for success in your own life.

Chapter 2: Lace Up Your Sneakers
Reframing Stressors into Opportunities

Anthony arrived at the tennis court early one Saturday morning, his tennis bag slung over his shoulder. The sun was just beginning to cast long shadows across the courts, and the air was filled with the sounds of tennis balls being hit and the occasional burst of laughter from the nearby park.

He was getting the hang of those court moves. Swings were smoother, steps more confident, but there was a sneaky little gremlin hanging around—a fear of making mistakes.

"Tennis is a game of failure," Coach Sarah declared, her eyes fixed on Anthony. Her statement hung in the air for a moment, leaving him slightly bewildered.

What did she mean by that?

Seeing the confusion in Anthony's eyes, she continued, "I want you to design a new drill for today, Anthony. But here's the catch: I want this drill to be all about failure."

Anthony furrowed his brow, unsure of what she was getting at. "Failure, Coach? Isn't the goal to win?"

Coach Sarah chuckled. "Winning is important, Anthony, but it's not the only goal. You see, every time you step onto this court, you will face failures—those shots you've missed, mistakes you've made, points you've lost. It's inevitable. The key to becoming a better player isn't avoiding failure; it's learning from it."

Anthony pondered her words for a moment. He had always seen failure as something to be ashamed of, as a sign that he wasn't good enough. But Coach Sarah was suggesting something different—a radical shift in perspective.

"Your drill should be designed to put you in situations where failure is likely," Coach Sarah continued, interrupting his thoughts. "I want you to confront it head-on and embrace it as a teacher. The more you fail in practice, the better you'll become at handling it in real matches."

Determined to understand this new approach, Anthony set to work designing a drill that focused on his weakest shots and most challenging game scenarios. He realized that he needed to create situations where failure was not just possible, but expected.

As the day went on, Anthony practiced his new drill, his racket sometimes missing the mark, and his shots landing far from their intended targets. But he wasn't disheartened. Instead, he analyzed each failure, trying to understand what had gone wrong and how he could improve.

Weeks turned into months, and Anthony continued to embrace failure as an essential part of his tennis journey. He became more resilient, identifying weaknesses, developing problem-solving skills, and reducing his fear of failure. Most importantly, he started to see that tennis was indeed a game of failure—but it was also a game of growth.

And then it occurred to him. What if it wasn't just tennis that was a game of failure? What if his work was as well? Could he apply this same approach to his job?

Anthony looked around his desk and all he could see was a pile of unfinished work. What was the root cause of his perpetual backlog? Ah, yes. It was his fear of making mistakes disguised as perfectionism. Deep down, he knew it was impossible to do a perfect job, but the fear led to avoidance. This strategy not only piled on the pressure, it did nothing to miraculously make the work disappear.

With a mix of reluctance and an unwavering determination, Anthony confronted his professional challenges with the same mindset he had honed on the tennis court — an attitude that embraced failure as a stepping stone toward personal growth. He examined his setbacks, pinpointed the chinks in his approach, and tirelessly sought innovative solutions. Armed with these newfound tactics, he zealously tackled his blueprints, contracts, and what had seemed to be an endless sea of paperwork.

To his astonishment, it worked. The evidence was tangible as the towering pile on his desk began to dwindle. Anthony had unearthed a valuable life lesson from this transformational experience. The prospect of failure did not have to be a menacing threat to be avoided at all costs. Rather, it was a gateway to personal growth and courage. It was as if a fog had lifted, revealing a path filled with opportunities he had previously overlooked.

Anthony now understood that, yes, sometimes he wouldn't get it right. There would be moments of imperfection, and that was perfectly okay. In fact, he saw these as valuable stepping stones on his journey toward improvement.

Embracing the possibility of failure meant he was taking risks, pushing boundaries, and testing his limits. It was like sowing the seeds of courage within himself, knowing that, even in those instances where he didn't quite hit the mark, he was increasing the chances of eventually getting things right, or at the very least, getting them done. And to Anthony, that realization made all the difference, infusing his work and life with newfound purpose and resilience.

Now it's your turn. Consider how reframing threats into challenges can benefit you. What unexplored horizons might lie just beyond your fear of failure?

Are there untapped opportunities awaiting your discovery? In pursuit of your aspirations, what daring leaps are you willing to take?

Chapter 3: Play Like a Champion

The Heartbeat of Purpose

As Anthony progressed through his tennis journey, he encountered yet another lesson that echoed far beyond the court's confines. This lesson wasn't about strategies or energy, but rather a profound understanding of himself and the nature of stress.

The revelation struck during a high-stakes practice match with Sarah. The sun beat down on the court, as the intensity in the air grew thicker. Anthony's every move was deliberate, every swing calculated. The score was tied, and the game seemed to hang in the balance.

As the ball sailed over the net, Anthony's heart pounded in rhythm with his determined steps. He swung his racket with all the fire of a competitor hell-bent on winning. But the ball didn't have enough lift and ended up hitting the net. "No!" Anthony exclaimed, looking devastated, his head hanging down.

The score remained at a deadlock, the tension ratcheting up as the moments ticked by. Anthony's eyes scanned the court, his mind racing, searching for that elusive opening.

Sarah, ever the astute observer, saw the storm brewing within Anthony. She stepped forward, her presence commanding attention. With a gentle but firm touch, she paused the game. Anthony's chest heaved as he caught his breath, the echoes of his frustration still hanging in the air.

And then, in a moment of clarity, Sarah's words cut through the tension. "Stress often surfaces when we truly care about something," she said simply, referring to the rollercoaster of emotions she was witnessing in front of her. Anthony's brow furrowed as he absorbed her words, the truth of them resonating within him.

Stress was a sign that he cared, that he had invested himself in the outcome. He understood that the same was true in his work. It wasn't merely about ego; it was rooted in his responsibility towards his employees, their families, and his own family's well-being. The success of his business had a ripple effect, and if it suffered, so did the livelihoods of those he cared about deeply.

As the realization settled in, Anthony's shoulders eased, his grip on the racket relaxing. Sarah's insight had unlocked a new perspective, revealing that stress wasn't an enemy to be defeated; it was a signpost of his devotion, a beacon that illuminated his commitment to the game. His heart still raced, but the tumultuous energy had transformed into a focused determination.

With a nod of gratitude, Anthony returned to the game. The ball flew across the net once again, but this time, he approached it with a blend of purpose and poise. His swing was powerful yet controlled, a testament to the equilibrium he had found within himself. The ball soared over the net, landing within the court, just beyond his opponent's reach.

The point was his, and the score tilted in his favor. But it wasn't just about winning the point; it was about the understanding that had been born from that moment of frustration.

This newfound perspective changed the way he approached stress. It became a signal of purpose, a reminder of his dedication and compassion. It didn't have to overwhelm him; rather, it could be a guide. With this realization, Anthony discovered a way to sidestep becoming entangled in the minutiae of daily tasks.

He anchored himself in his sense of purpose, staying focused on what truly mattered. The "why" behind his actions gave him clarity amidst chaos.

However, this realization also brought to light a disheartening truth. Over the years, while striving for success, he had moved away from what he believed in the most. Instead of taking care of his family relationships, he had become stuck in the relentless demands of his business. This big realization led to a big change. He began to delegate tasks, so the workload wasn't all on him. He reclaimed his weekends, spending more time with his family instead of tethering himself to his laptop. And when watching sports, like tennis matches, he focused on being with his family rather than thinking about work.

Take a moment to reflect on the parallels between Anthony's journey and your own life. Think about what really matters to you. When stress shows up, it might mean you care deeply. Remember, you can use that as a sign to stay on track and not get overwhelmed. When you have a clear reason for what you do, you won't get lost in the small stuff. Take time for what's important and be present in those moments.

Chapter 4: Game Set Match

Lessons of Resilience

As Anthony's journey through tennis and stress unfolded, he discovered three powerful lessons that transformed his perspective on stress. The first lesson taught him to reframe stressors from threats to opportunities, even in the toughest situations. The second lesson showed him that stress can be a source of energy and focus, a sign that he's ready to tackle whatever comes his way. The third lesson revealed that stress arises from caring deeply about something, and it's a reminder to stay aligned with his purpose.

Throughout his journey, Anthony not only applied these principles on the tennis court but also in the broader arena of life. Consequently, his tennis game improved, but his approach to work, his relationships, and the world around him transformed.

Anthony's wife, Emily, had always known him to be the hardworking, perfectionist husband who dedicated himself to his work with unwavering commitment. She saw how his pursuit of excellence often led to sleepless nights, endless piles of paperwork, and an unrelenting drive to succeed. She, too, had felt the weight of their hectic life, as a mother of 3 young children and a career.

But as Anthony delved deeper into his journey of stress management through tennis, Emily began to notice a change. The late-night calls from the office grew less frequent. The once perfectionist tendencies that caused him to stress over every minor detail began to wane. Instead, she witnessed a newfound sense of ease and balance in her husband.

He started delegating tasks at work, trusting his team to handle things without micromanaging. He began setting boundaries, allowing himself personal time, and, most importantly, appreciating the moments they shared as a family.

Emily couldn't help but smile as she observed these transformations. The man she loved was evolving, not into someone different, but into a version of himself that had been buried beneath the stress and perfectionism for so long. She saw the twinkle in his eyes return, the relaxed posture that had been absent for years, and a newfound zest for life.

As the days turned into weeks and then months, Anthony's changes became even more evident. His once frantic pace had slowed, and he was no longer perpetually on the verge of burnout. Emily, on the other hand, found herself in familiar territory, still juggling the relentless demands of her own busy life.

It was only when Anthony looked at his wife, her eyes reflecting the same chaos he had once felt, that he realized just how far he had come. The stress that had once consumed him had now become a challenge he could conquer, a game he had learned to play. And as he stood by Emily's side, he vowed to share the lessons he had learned, not just on the tennis court but in the arena of life itself.

Now, I want to challenge you to apply these principles in your own life. When stress knocks on your door, remember the lessons Anthony learned on the tennis court. Harness the surge of energy that stress provides to stay focused and precise. Reframe challenges as chances for growth. Recognize that stress is a sign that you care.

Reflect on times when stress felt overwhelming. How can you channel the energy it brings to enhance your focus and performance? Can you find the opportunity within the challenge? And, most importantly, what aspects of your life resonate with such deep care that stress is inevitable? Embrace these challenges with a new perspective, just like Anthony did, and watch how your relationship with stress transforms into a source of strength and resilience.

As you navigate the intricate dance between stress and growth, remember that the power to channel, reframe, and care lies within you. It's not about erasing stress, but about embracing it as a vital part of your journey. Just as a tennis player transforms their game through practice and strategy, you too can reshape your relationship with stress and move forward with purpose and confidence.

The Stress Advantage

Sharon Grossman, Ph.D.

OTHER BOOKS BY DR. SHARON

The 7E Solution to Burnout: Transforming High Achievers from Exhausted to Extraordinary

How to Train Your Brain for Success in 5 Steps

The Stress Advantage

SPEAKER I AUTHOR I TRAINER

Dr. Sharon Grossman is an international keynote speaker and workshop leader who teaches organizations how to keep their employees happier working for them than their competition. Through her signature talks on managing stress and boosting productivity, Sharon equips her audiences with practical tools and strategies to navigate the challenges of modern life. Her insights are grounded in cutting-edge research, neuroscience, and emotional intelligence, making her presentations both evidence-based and incredibly impactful.

Sharon is the brain behind The Productivity Trainers, a corporate training company geared towards transforming overwhelmed teams into high performers.

To book a chat with Dr. Sharon for speaking, training or consulting, go to: http://drsharongrossman.com/bookme

SPEAKING TESTIMONIALS

Sharon is one of the great speakers I heard about beating burnout.

Blenda Larioza, Registered Nurse Alberta Health Services

I always knew what my mindset was capable of, but Sharon's session taught me how to access my capability in a more in-depth manner from a new direction of thinking.

Debra Mcdougall, Psychologist University of Calgary

Extremely motivational! We all get stuck and this allowed us to take a step back and recognize it and take action moving forward!

Carianne Giersch, Customer Success Manager Athena Health

Sharon's presentation was engaging and full of tools to help people deal with anxiety, stress and burnout. I would highly recommend Sharon as a speaker at conferences and to all levels and areas of your organizations.

Alan Vanderburg, Consultant Manager Tulsa County

Sharon Grossman, Ph.D.

The Stress Advantage

Sharon Grossman, Ph.D.

www.ingramcontent.com/pod-product-compliance
Lightning Source LLC
Chambersburg PA
CBHW032005060426
42449CB00031B/706